AMERICAN MEDICINAL FLOWERS

US DEPARTMENT OF AGRICULTURE BULLETIN 26

First Edition 1913
Alice Henkel

New Edition 2019
Edited by Tarl Warwick
Illustrations by Rita Metzner

COPYRIGHT AND DISCLAIMER

FOREWORD

This little booklet is one of a number of agricultural circulars produced by the US government at the start of the 20th century in an effort to maximize the production of medically active plants (often pestilent weeds of no other value) for domestic use or export. Efforts such as these were joined with general land improvement efforts and attempts made to make even the removal of noxious species useful to farmers.

The species listed here are quite common; I cannot recommend any of the medical usages here, as they have been supplanted by more modern medical practices, but some species (datura notably) are indeed active on a medicinal level; a hundred years ago, treatment often included nothing more than fighting symptoms, as the case is here with mustard plasters and berry syrups. The occultist should have at least a basic and preferably an advanced knowledge of plant and fungi species, and their various usages in the sense of woodcraft for the purposes of ritual, survival, or mere interest and sport. Here, we see the 20th century fixation with standardization replacing the 19th century fixation with mere receipts and preparations, often supplied in massive volumes with hundreds or even thousands of individual compounds and tinctures.

This edition of "American Medicinal Flowers" has been carefully edited for format and content. Care has been taken to retain all original intent and meaning.

AMERICAN MEDICINAL FLOWERS

INTRODUCTION

While the greater number of plants employed for medicinal purposes are valued for their roots, barks, or leaves, some are useful on account of their flowers, fruits, or seeds. Such flowers, fruits, and seeds as seem to be in greatest demand at present are included in this bulletin, and of the 13 mentioned 6 are listed as official in the Eighth Decennial Revision of the United States Pharmacopoeia.

COLLECTION OF FLOWERS, FRUITS, AND SEEDS

Flowers bring the best price when, after drying, they retain as nearly as possible their natural color and odor. They should be gathered when they first open, or at least very soon afterwards, and no faded flowers must be included. In seeking to preserve the natural color the flowers should be carefully dried in the shade and prevented from becoming moist. Fruits or berries should be gathered at maturity and must be very carefully dried, so that they may not adhere to each other or become moldy.

Seeds should be collected as they are ripening, just before the seed pods open or as they are about to open. They may be placed in trays and dried in the open air and shaken frequently to insure drying throughout. Bits of stems or leaves or shriveled seeds should, of course, be removed.

When ready for shipment each lot may be carefully packed in sound burlap bags or in clean boxes. Samples should previously have been sent to drug dealers for their inspection, who should be informed also as to the quantity the prospective seller has to dispose of.

AMERICAN MEDICINAL FLOWERS

Only approximate prices are mentioned herein for the purpose of giving the collector some idea concerning the possible range. Prices are constantly fluctuating, and it is therefore not possible to make any definite statement regarding them. Correspondence with drug dealers will bring the desired information in this respect.

The medicinal uses are referred to only very briefly, and the statements made regarding such uses are based on information contained in various dispensaries and kindred publications. The bulletin herewith
is not intended to give medical advice; this should be sought only from a physician.

PLANTS FURNISHING MEDICINAL FLOWERS, FRUITS, AND SEEDS

Under each section are included the synonyms and pharmacopceial name, if any, the common names, habitat, range, descriptions, and information in regard to the collection, prices, and uses of the parts in question.

JUNIPER

Juniperus communis L.

Other common names: Fairy circle, hackmatack, horse savin, gorst, aiten.

Habitat and range: The juniper is of common occurrence on dry, sterile hills from Canada south to New Jersey, west to Nebraska, and in the Rocky Mountains to New Mexico.

Description: Juniper is an evergreen shrub belonging to the pine family (Pinaceae), sometimes attaining the height of a small tree, with erect trunk and spreading branches, covered with a shreddy bark. The spreading leaves are borne in whorls of three and are straight and rigid, about one-fourth to one-half (rarely three-fourths) of an inch in length, awl shaped, with a sharp, prickly point; above they are grooved and of a bright green color, while; underneath they are whitish.

Fig. 1: Juniper (*Juniperus communis*), leafy branches and fruit.

The flowers are of two kinds, male and female, and are generally produced on separate plants, in April or May, the male flowers being borne in short, oval catkins, while the female flowers are arranged in a short cone, consisting of about five overlapping whorls. The fleshy, berrylike fruit which follows does not ripen until the second year. It is dark purple, covered with a pale-bluish bloom, roundish, and contains three bony seeds embedded in a brownish pulp. (Fig. 1.)

Collection, uses, and prices: The berries are used medicinally and should be collected when ripe, usually about October. They have an aromatic, somewhat spicy odor, and a pungent, turpentine-like, bitterish sweet taste. An oil, known as oil of juniper, is distilled from them, and is official in the Pharmacopoeia of the United States. The oil content seems to vary according to the sections from which the berries are obtained. Most of the juniper berries of commerce come from the southern portions of Europe. Juniper berries are employed medicinally for their stimulant and diuretic properties. They are used also for flavoring gin. The price at present paid for juniper berries is about 2 to 1.5 cents a pound.

SAW PALMETTO

Serenoa serrulata (Michx.) Hook. f.

Pharmacopceial name: Sabal.

Synonym: Sabalserrulatum Roem. and Schult.

Other common names: Palmetto, dwarf palmetto, fan palm.

Habitat and range: This palm is found in sandy soil from North Carolina and Arkansas to Florida and Texas.

Description: The saw palmetto is a fan-leaved palm, low and tufted, with a creeping, branching stem 4 to 8 feet long. The bright-green leaves are borne on a slender stalk edged with spines and are roundish in outline and fan shaped, the 15 to 30 divisions or segments slightly cleft at the top. (Fig. 2.) The spike (spadix) is thickly hairy, considerably shorter than the leaves, and the flowers are small and whitish. The fruit or drupe is oblong oval, about one half to scarcely 1 inch in length. 1-seeded like an olive, reddish brown or blackish brown, and smooth, but somewhat wrinkled in drying. This plant belongs to the palm family (Phoenicaceae).

Collection, uses, and prices: The partially dried ripe fruit is the part used in medicine and is official in the United States Pharmacopoeia. The fruit ripens from October to December, but its collection is begun as early as August, before maturity, and extends into January. It is said to improve digestion and is also used for neuralgic troubles and for allaying irritation of the mucous membranes. Saw-palmetto berries now bring about 25 to 27 cents a pound.

Fig. 2: Saw palmetto (*Serenoa serrulata*), showing creeping stem.

WORMSEED

Chenopodium anthelminticum L.

Synonym: Chenopodium ambrosioides anthelminticum A. Gray.

Other common names: Chenopodium, American wormseed, Jerusalem oak.

Habitat and range: Wormseed has been naturalized in this country from tropical America and occurs in waste places from New England to Florida and westward to California.

Description: This common weed is an annual or sometimes a perennial belonging to the goosefoot family (Chenopodiacea) and it has a smoothish, much branched stem about 2 to 3 feet in height and oblong or lance-shaped leaves. The margins of the leaves are wavy toothed or almost unbroken. The lower leaves are about 1 to 3 inches long, the numerous upper leaves being much smaller and usually tapering at both ends. The greenish flowers are produced from about July to September, in crowded spikes mixed with leaves, and are followed by small, green, and roundish fruits. The entire plant has a strong, disagreeable odor, due to the essential oil which it contains. The fruits likewise have a very powerful odor. (Fig. 3.)

Collection, prices, and uses: The fruits are the part employed medicinally and were official in the Pharmacopoeia for 1890. They are in the form of small grains, round but slightly flattened, about the size of a pinhead, and enclosing the small, shining black seeds. They have a green color and a disagreeable, strong, and penetrating odor which does not diminish in drying. The fruit is distilled for the oil. which it contains in large quantities. In the United States Pharmacopoeia for 1890 the fruit alone was directed to be used for the distillation of the oil, but the entire leafy part is sometimes employed for this purpose. Wormseed is cultivated to a considerable extent in parts of Maryland, where the distillation of the plant for the oil is carried on. Wormseed is used in medicine as an anthelmintic, that is, for expelling worms.

The price of wormseed at present ranges from about 8 to

10 cents a pound, and oil of wormseed is quoted at from $2.25 to $2.50 a pound, wholesale.

Fig. 3: Wormseed (*Chenopodium anthelminticum*) fruiting branches.

POKEWEED

Phytolacca americana L.

Synonym: Phytolacca dacandra L.

Common names: Poke, Virginian poke, pigeon berry, garget, scoke, pocan, coakum, inkberry, red inkberry, American nightshade, cancer jalap, redweed.

Habitat and range: Pokeweed is common in rich, moist soil along fences, margins of fields, and in uncultivated land from New England to Minnesota, south to Florida and Texas. It has been naturalized in Europe and is there regarded as an ornamental.

Description: The large perennial root of pokeweed sends up stout, smooth, erect, and branched stems from 3 to 9 feet in height, which at first are green and then reddish. Its leaves are rather large, smooth, and borne on short stems; they measure about 5 inches in length and 2 to 3 inches in width, ovate or ovate oblong in outline, pointed at the apex, and with unbroken margins. Numerous whitish flowers are produced from about July to September, borne on reddish stems in long-stalked clusters about 3 to 4 inches in length, followed by dark-purple berries.

Poke berries are roundish, flattened at both ends, smooth and shining, and contain black seeds embedded in a rich, crimson juice. (Fig. 4.) Pokeweed belongs to the pokeweed family (Phytolaceaceae).

Fig. 4: Pokeweed (*Phytolacca americana*), flowering and fruiting branches, also root and section of root.

Collection, uses, and prices: The berries are collected when fully mature, about two months after flowering, and the clusters carefully dried in the shade. Poke berries have no odor, and the taste at first is sweetish, then acrid. They are poisonous. Used medicinally they have alterative properties and are used in treating various diseases of the skin and blood; they act upon the bowels and also cause vomiting. The root is likewise used in medicine and is at present official in the United States Pharmacopoeia. The price of poke berries ranges from 3 to 4 cents a pound.

BLACK MUSTARD

Brassica nigra (L.) Koch.

Pharmacopaeial name: Sinapis nigra.

Synonym: Sinapis nigra L.

Other common names: Red mustard, brown mustard, cadlock, kerlock. Senvre, scurvy.

Habitat and range: Black mustard has been introduced from Europe and is a common weed in cultivated ground and waste places almost throughout the United States, being especially troublesome in grain fields and pastures. Both black and white mustards are cultivated on a commercial scale in California.

Description: The lower part of the stems and branches of black mustard is more or less covered with bristly hairs, while the upper portion of the rather stiff green stem is usually smooth. Black mustard, which is an annual belonging to the mustard family (Brassicaceae), grows about 2 to 6 feet in height.

It has dark-green leaves, rough with bristly hairs. The lower leaves are slender stemmed, deeply lobed, the terminal lobe being the largest and the two or more lateral ones smaller, the margin toothed all around. The leaves toward the top of the plant are shorter stemmed or stemless and are lance shaped and slightly toothed.

The bright-yellow flowers appear in clusters at the ends of the stems and are produced from about June to September. The flowers measure scarcely a quarter of an inch in diameter and consist of four spreading petals, each with a rounded blade and narrow claw. Alternating with the petals are the pale green sepals or calyx lobes. Numerous erect pods are produced from July to November, crowded against the stem in dense, narrow clusters. The pods are narrowly linear, about an inch in length and four sided, smooth, with a slender beak at the apex. The seeds contained in the pods are very numerous, small and roundish, blackish or reddish brown, and finely pitted.

Collection, uses, and prices: When the pods are nearly ripe, but before they are ready to burst open, the tops may be pulled. These pods should then be placed on a clean, dry floor or shelf, allowing them to mature and dry out. when they will spring open and the seeds can be shaken out. Black mustard seeds are official in the United States Pharmacopoeia.

When collected, or even when it is powdered in its dry state, mustard has no odor whatever, but as soon as water is added when it is ground the strong, penetrating mustard odor is developed. Mustard has a sharp and pungent taste. Black mustard is very much used as a counter-irritant, being applied to painful surfaces in the form of a poultice, causing reddening of the skin and blistering if kept on too long. It is also used internally for its emetic and laxative action. Black-mustard seed brings about 2 to 4 cents a pound.

WHITE MUSTARD

Sinapis alba L.

Pharmacopoeial, name: Sinapis alba.

Other common names: Yellow mustard, charlock, kedlock, senvre.

Habitat and range: White mustard is a weed, naturalized from Europe and found in cultivated fields and waste places, but not so abundant nor so widely distributed as the black mustard. It is cultivated on a commercial scale in California.

Description: This annual plant, while much resembling the black mustard, is smaller, reaching only about 1 to 2 feet in height, and is also of a brighter green color. It is more or less hairy, with stiff, spreading hairs. The lower leaves are 6 to 8 inches in length, with toothed margins, deeply lobed, the divisions reaching to the midrib, the terminal lobe large, and those at the sides smaller. The upper leaves are lance shaped and somewhat toothed. The surface of the leaves is rough hairy. The flowers are considerably larger than those of black mustard and of a lighter yellow color. The pods are rough hairy, contracted between seeds, and have a long beak. In the white mustard these pods are spreading, instead of being pressed against the stem as is the case in black mustard, and the seed, which is roundish, pale yellowish, and very minutely pitted, is also larger. (Fig. 5.)

Collection, uses, and prices: The seeds, which are official in the United States Pharmacopoeia, are collected in the same manner as those of black mustard; that is, the fruiting tops should be gathered before they are fully ripe and placed in a clean place to mature and dry, after which the seeds can be easily shaken out.

White-mustard seed is likewise used in the preparation of plasters and poultices, and internally for its laxative and emetic properties. Like black mustard, these seeds do not develop the mustard odor until water is added when they are ground, but it is not as pronounced in these, neither is the taste as pungent. The price is about the same as for black mustard, ranging from 2 to 4 cents a pound.

Fig. 5: White mustard (*Sinapis alba*) plant, showing flowers and seed pods.

RASPBERRIES

(1) *Rubus occidentals L.,* and (2) *Rubus strigosus* Michx.

Synonyms: (1) Rubus idaeus var. americanus Torr.; (2) Rubus idaeus var. strigosus Maxim.

Other common names: (1) Black raspberry, thimbleberry, blackcap, Scotch cap, wild purple raspberry; (2) wild red raspberry, American red raspberry.

Habitat and range: The black raspberry (R. occidentalis) grows along the borders of woods and in rocky thickets from Canada south to Georgia and Missouri, while the red raspberry (R. strigosus) is found in dry or rocky situations from Canada to North Carolina and New Mexico.

Descriptions: The raspberries are so well known that a full description seems unnecessary. However, the black raspberry has recurved, cane-like stems, which root at the tips and are covered with a bloom. These canes sometimes reach 12 feet in length and are furnished with hooked prickles. The leaves consist generally of three leaflets, oval in outline, pointed, and coarsely double toothed, whitish hairy underneath. The black raspberry is in flower about May to June, and the well-known purplish black fruit ripens in July.

The wild red raspberry is a more shrubby plant, about 3 to 6 feet in height, its stems being thickly furnished with bristles. The leaflets, three to five in number, are oval or oval oblong, long pointed, sharply toothed, and measure about 1 to 3 inches in length and are also whitish hairy on the lower surface. It is in flower from about May to July and ripens its light red fruit from July to September. Both species are found in cultivation.

Raspberries belong to the rose family (Rosaceae).

Collection, uses, and prices: The fruits of these plants are collected when ripe and are used for their refrigerant and somewhat laxative properties. Their chief use, however, is to furnish a syrup. By allowing the juice of the fruit to ferment, a pleasant wine is obtained, which is much used in a domestic way for bowel complaints. The wholesale price of dried raspberries may range from 25 to 30 cents or more a pound.

PRICKLY ASH

(1) *Zanthoxylum americanum* Mill., and (2) *Zanthoxylum clavaherculis* L.

Synonyms: (1) Zanthoxylum fraxineum Willd ; (2) Zantlioxylum carolinianum Lam.; Fagara clava-herculis (L.) Small.

Other common names: (1) Northern prickly ash, toothache tree, toothache bush, yellowwood, angelica tree, pellitory bark, suterberry; (2) southern prickly ash, toothache tree, Hercules' club, yellow Hercules, yellowthorn, yellowwood, yellow prickly ash. prickly yellowwood, West Indian yellowwood, sea ash, pepperwood, wild orange.

Habitat and range: The northern prickly ash is found along river banks, in woods and thickets, from Virginia, Missouri, and Nebraska northward to Canada; the southern prickly ash occurs along streams from southern Virginia to Florida, west to Texas and Arkansas.

Description: Both of these species are native in this country and are members of the rue family (Rutacea). The northern prickly ash is not a large tree, rarely exceeding 25 feet in height, and is most frequently found reaching only 10 to 12 feet, its branches being furnished with brown, cone-shaped prickles. The leaves consist of from 5 to 11 oval, practically stemless leaflets 1.5 to 2 inches long, with somewhat pointed apex and wavy-toothed or unbroken margins; they are dark green above and paler green underneath. The leaflets are somewhat hairy when young, but later they become smooth or, at least, are only slightly hairy. About April or May, before the leaves are out, the greenish yellow flowers appear, crowded together in small stemless clusters in the axils of the branches.

The seed capsules are roundish or somewhat oval, wrinkled or pitted, greenish red, and with a lemon odor. One or two shining black seeds are contained in each capsule. The southern prickly ash is generally taller than the northern, but rarely exceeds 45 feet in height, and sometimes occurs only as a shrub. The bark of the trunk is of a slate-gray color, and the entire tree is covered with sharp spines. All of these spines have broad corky bases, which on the trunk remain after the spines or prickles have fallen away. The spines on the leaf stems and branches are larger than those of the trunk.

Fig. 6: Southern Prickly ash. (*Zanthoxylum Clavaherculis*) leaves, fruits, and branches showing prickles.

The leaves consist of 5 to 17 leaflets, 1 to 3 inches long, ovate lance shaped in outline, pointed at the top, and with uneven sides furnished with wavy-toothed margin; the upper surface is smooth and shining and the lower side dull. The numerous small, greenish white flowers are produced after the leaves have appeared, in large clusters at the ends of the branches, not in the axils of the leaves as in the northern prickly ash. The wrinkled seed capsules are roundish obovoid and contain roundish oblong, black, and coarsely wrinkled seeds. (Fig. 6.)

Collection, uses, and prices: The berries are gathered at time of maturity. As found in the stores they consist of the open, valved, brownish capsules, sometimes with the seed still enclosed, but generally it has shattered out. They have an aromatic odor, a pungent, aromatic taste, and are used medicinally for their stimulant, carminative, and antispasmodic properties.

The bark of both of the foregoing species is employed medicinally and is at present official in the United States Pharmacopoeia. The present wholesale price of prickly-ash berries is quoted at 19 cents a pound.

SMOOTH SUMAC

Rhus glabra L.

Pharmacopoeial name: Rhus glabra.

Other common names: Mountain sumac, upland sumac, scarlet sumac, sleek sumac, white sumac, Pennsylvania sumac, shoe-make, vinegar tree, senhalanac.

Habitat and range: Smooth sumac occurs in dry soil, thickets, and waste grounds nearly throughout the United States and Canada.

Description: Although sometimes attaining the height of a small tree, the smooth sumac is more frequently found as a rather handsome shrub 2 to 12 feet high, with smooth, brownish gray trunk and branches. It belongs to the sumac family (Anacardiacese) and is an indigenous perennial. Its leaves are very long, from 1 to 3 feet, and consist of from 11 to 31 leaflets, each leaflet being about 2 to 4 inches in length and about half as wide. The leaflets are thin in texture, lance shaped, with a long-pointed apex and rounded base, and sharply toothed margins; they are smooth, dark green on the upper surface, and whitish underneath. Smooth sumac is in flower from June to August, the greenish yellow flowers being borne in large, dense pyramidal clusters at the ends of the branches. The fruit is flattened roundish, and covered with short, crimson hairs, which are very sour. Each fruit or berry contains a smooth, 1 seeded stone. (Fig. 7.)

Collection, uses, and prices: The dried fruit of the smooth sumac is official in the United States Pharmacopoeia and should be gathered while the downy covering is still on the berries, which gives to them their acid taste. They have no odor, but are very acid and astringent. Their principal use seems to be as a gargle in inflamed throat. The bark is also used in medicine. The berries bring about 5 cents a pound.

Fig. 7: Smooth sumac (*Rhus glabra*), of fruits, leaves and cluster

AMERICAN MEDICINAL FLOWERS

AMERICAN LINDEN

Tilia americana L.

Synonyms: Tilia glabra Vent.; Tilia canadensis Michx.

Other common names: Basswood. whitewood, bast tree, black lime tree, American lin tree, American lime tree, bee tree, daddynut tree, monkeynut tree, whistlewood, white lind, red basswood, yellow basswood, wickup.

Habitat and range: This native forest tree is found in rich woods, especially along the mountains, from Canada to Georgia, west to Texas and Nebraska.

Description: The American linden attains great size, from 60 to 125 feet in height, with a trunk diameter of 2 to 5 feet, and spreading branches. The leaves are somewhat leathery in texture, smooth on both sides or sometimes hairy on the veins of the under side. They are obliquely oval in outline, with sharply toothed margin, pointed at the apex, and heart shaped at the base, and are borne on stems about an inch or two in length.

From about May to June the tree is loaded with drooping clusters of 6 to 20 yellowish, very fragrant flowers. At the base of each flower cluster and partly grown to it is a large bract (or leaflike part) 2 to 4 inches in length, very pale green, and strongly veined. The fruit is roundish, greenish gray; dry and woody, and contains one or two seeds. (Fig. 8.) This tree belongs to the linden family (Tiliaceae).

Collection, uses, and prices: The flowers are the parts employed medicinally. These are collected in May or June and carefully dried in the shade. The very sweet odor is lost in drying. The taste is mucilaginous and sweetish.

An infusion of the flowers has been very much used as a domestic remedy for headaches, indigestion, and for breaking up colds. The flowers of other species of linden are also employed. Linden flowers at present are quoted at 35 cents a pound.

Fig. 8. American linden (*Tilia americana,*), leaves, flowers, and fruits.

POISON HEMLOCK

Conium maculatum L.

Pharmacopoeial name: Conium.

Other common names: Spotted parsley, spotted cowbane, poison parsley. St. Bennet's-herb, bad-man's-oatmeal, wode-whistle, cashes, bunk, heck-how, poison root, spotted hemlock, spotted conium, poison snakeweed, beaver poison.

Habitat and range: Naturalized in this country from

Europe, this poisonous weed is now rather common in waste places and along roadsides, principally in the Eastern and Middle States.

Description: Poison hemlock is a very dangerous weed, the close resemblance of the leaves to those of parsley often causing it to be mistaken for the latter, with fatal results, all parts of the plant being extremely poisonous. It belongs to the parsley family (Apiaceae).

It is a biennial plant, with hollow, smooth, purple-spotted stem about 2 to 6 feet in height, much branched, and large, parsleylike leaves. About June or July rather showy, flat topped clusters of numerous small, white flowers are produced, measuring about 1 to 3 inches across. The fruit, which ripens in August and September, is grayish green, about one-eighth of an inch in length, ovate, flattened on the sides, and ribbed. (Fig. 9.)

The entire plant has a disagreeable mouselike odor, which becomes especially noticeable when the plant is bruised.

Collection, uses, and prices: The fruit of the poison hemlock is official in the United States Pharmacopoeia, and must yield, when assayed by the pharmacopoeial process, not less than 5 per cent of conin. It should be collected while still green but full grown, about August or September, carefully dried in a dark but well-ventilated place, and stored in tight cans or boxes so that no light or air can reach it. The odor is not very pronounced, except when the fruit has been bruised, when the mousy odor becomes noticeable. The taste is disagreeable and somewhat acrid. Poison hemlock is not fit to be used after having been kept for more than two years. It is a very poisonous drug and is used in excited conditions of the nervous system and in rheumatism, neuralgia, and asthma. The leaves of the poison hemlock are also employed medicinally.

Poison hemlock fruits bring about 8 to 9 cents a pound.

Fig. 9: Poison hemlock (*Conium maculatum*) leaves, flowers, and fruits.

JIMSON WEED

Datura stramonium L.

Other common names: Stramonium, Jamestown weed, Jamestown lily, thorn apple, devil's-apple, devil's-trumpet, mad-apple, apple of Peru, stinkweek, stink, fireweed, dewtry.

Habitat and range: Jimson weed is a common plant of fields and waste places, occurring throughout the country, with the exception of the North and West. It is native in the Tropics and widely scattered in nearly all warm countries.

Description: This very common, ill-scented weed is a poisonous plant belonging to the nightshade family (Solanaceae).

It is an annual of rather rank growth, with stout, yellowish green stems about 2 to 5 feet high, much forked and leafy. The thin, smooth leaves are veiny, dark green above and paler green on the under surface, and rather large, measuring from 3 to 8 inches in length; the apex is pointed and the margins are irregularly waved and toothed, usually narrowing toward the base. Jimson weed produces rather large, showy flowers from about May to September, each measuring about 3 inches in length, white and funnel shaped, and having a strong odor. The seed pod consists of a dry, oval, prickly capsule, which when ripe bursts open into four valves containing numerous seeds having a disagreeable odor when fresh. The seeds are dull black, about one-sixth of an inch in length, kidney shaped, flattened, wrinkled, and marked with small depressions. (Fig. 10.)

Fig. 10: Jimson weed (*Datura stramonium*), leaves, flowers, and seed pods.

Collection, uses, and prices: For the collection of the seeds the capsules should be cut from the plants when fully ripe but still green. These capsules or seed pods should then be dried and after a few days they will burst open, when the seeds can be readily shaken out. The seeds should now be thinly spread out and carefully dried. Jimson weed or stramonium seeds are poisonous, like the leaves, and are used principally in asthmatic troubles. They bring about 6 to 7 cents a pound. The leaves are also used medicinally and are official in the United States Pharmacopoeia.

MULLEIN

Verbascum thapsus L.

Other common names: Common mullein, great mullein, mullein dock, velvet dock, Aaron's-rod. Adam's flannel, old-mans flannel, blanket-leaf, bullock's lungwort, cow's lungwort, clown's lungwort, candlewick, feltwort, flannel-leaf, hare's beard, hedge taper, hog taper, ice-leaf, Jacob's staff, Jupiter's-staff, lady's foxglove. Peter's staff, shepherd's club, torches, torchwort, velvet plant, woollen.

Habitat and range: Mullein is a weed found in fields, pastures, along roadsides, and in waste places, its range extending from Maine to Minnesota and southward. It is also spreading in the Western States.

Description: It is not a difficult matter to recognize this plant, with its tall, straight stem, its large felty or flannel-like leaves, and its long, dense spike of yellow flowers. (Fig. 11.)

Mullein is a member of the figwort family (Scrophulariacea) and is a biennial, producing during its first year only a rosette of downy leaves, followed from June to August of the second year by the long flowering stalk with its close clusters of golden-yellow flowers. The stout, densely hairy, erect stem of the mullein plant reaches a height sometimes of 7 feet. The leaves, which, with the exception of the basal ones, are stemless, are placed alternately along the stem: they are from 4 to 12 inches in length, thick and rough, with dense, felty hairs above and below, oblong in outline and pointed at the top, their margins extending winglike down the stem. The sulfur-colored corolla of the mullein flowers is wheel shaped and five lobed, with rounded, somewhat unequal lobes, and, as stated, the flowers are densely crowded in an elongated, cylindrical, narrow spike. They have a honey-like odor.

Collection, uses, and prices: The flowers are used medicinally, that is, the corolla, the other parts being discarded. These are collected when about fully open, but before the petals are ready to drop. They have a sweetish odor and a mucilaginous, sweet taste. Mullein is used for the relief of coughs and catarrhs and also in diarrheal complaints. The leaves are similarly employed. Mullein flowers are listed wholesale at from 70 to 80 cents a pound.

Fig. 11: Mullein (*Verbascum Thapsus*) Flowering plant.

ELDER

Sambucus canadensis L.

Other common names: American elder, sweet elder, sambucus, elder flowers, elder blows.

Habitat and range: The elder bush is found in rich soil and low, somewhat damp ground from Canada southward to Florida and Arizona.

Description: Elder is an indigenous shrub and is a member of the honeysuckle family (Caprifoliaceae).

The deliciously sweet odor given off by the large flat clusters of creamy white flowers when the bush is in full bloom is well known. The shrub attains a height of 6 to 10 feet, its light-gray, numerous stems being generally smooth and the younger ones containing a large white pith. The leaves are rather large and consist of 5 to 11 oval leaflets borne on short stalks; these are pointed at the apex, smooth above and somewhat hairy on the veins beneath, and measure from about 2 to 5 inches in length, with margins sharply toothed. About June or July the flat-topped, fragrant clusters appear, composed of numerous small, five-lobed, wheel-shaped, creamy white flowers.

The clusters of edible fruits which follow are black or a very dark purple, small, round, shining, and juicy. (Fig. 12.)

Collection, uses, and prices: The flowers and fruits are used in medicine, the flowers having been official in the United States Pharmacopoeia for 1890. The flowers should be collected when fully opened and then quickly dried. They should have a nice yellowish color when dry, not a brownish or black appearance.

Fig. 12. Elder (*Sambucus canadensis*) Leaves, flowering and fruiting clusters.

The odor is not very strong in the dried flowers and the taste is mucilaginous and somewhat bitter. Elder flowers are used as a household remedy for their diuretic and diaphoretic properties and for poultices and ointments in the treatment of rheumatism, sores, burns, etc. The berries are occasionally used for their cooling, aperient, and diuretic properties. The inner bark is likewise sometimes employed in medicine. Elder flowers at present bring about 18 to 20 cents a pound.

THE END

www.ingramcontent.com/pod-product-compliance
Lightning Source LLC
Chambersburg PA
CBHW050758250726
48662CB00005B/2290